The Sacred H

Color-and-Learn Book

MW01070607

Outline by Father Francis Larkin, SS.CC.
Text by Sister John Mary, S.S.N.D.
Illustrations by Sister John Vianney, S.S.N.D.
Illustration Edited by Nicole M. McGinnis

St. Jerome Library

WWW.STJEROMELIBRARY.ORG

ISBN 978-1724690319

COPYRIGHT ©2018 BY ST. JEROME LIBRARY PRESS

ELKHORN, WI

When we say "Sacred Heart of Jesus" we mean that He loves us very much. Jesus wants you to love Him and get others to love Him. We will tell you more about that in this book.

With Love from God

God made all things
just because He loves us.

Dear God, thank You
for Your love for me!

Jesus became a little child like me
just because He loves us.

Jesus suffered
and died . . .

just because He loves us.

Jesus loves us so much that He wants to be with us always. The night before He died, He gave us a wonderful gift. He gave us Himself in the white Host.

8

No one loves us as much as Jesus does. But there are people who do not love Jesus. Jesus says, "Love Me to make up for all those who do not love Me!" Jesus chose Margaret Mary to tell this to everyone.

Margaret Mary was a little French girl who loved Jesus very much. She tried to show her love by talking to Jesus every day . . .

. . . by teaching children
to love and please Jesus,
and by helping
others in every way.

. . . by doing her chores
because she loved Jesus.

When Margaret Mary grew up, she became a Sister. One day Jesus came to her. He was very sad. Jesus said, "Behold this Heart which loves all men so much. But they do not love Me. See how they offend Me! Each thorn in My Heart is from saying NO to Me."

Jesus says: "Come, receive Me often in Holy Communion. Come, visit Me in church. I am waiting for you."

Jesus promised: "If you receive Me on the nine First Fridays, I will be with you when you die."

"Dear Jesus. I love You so much! I love You for those who do not love You."

"Jesus, I'm sorry for offending You."

Jesus wants you to help Him be King of _your_ home and every home. This true story will tell you how to do it.

A long time ago a little boy named Tarcisius was carrying Jesus in the Sacred Host to some Christians in prison. On the way he met some boys who hated Jesus. They tried to take Jesus away from him.

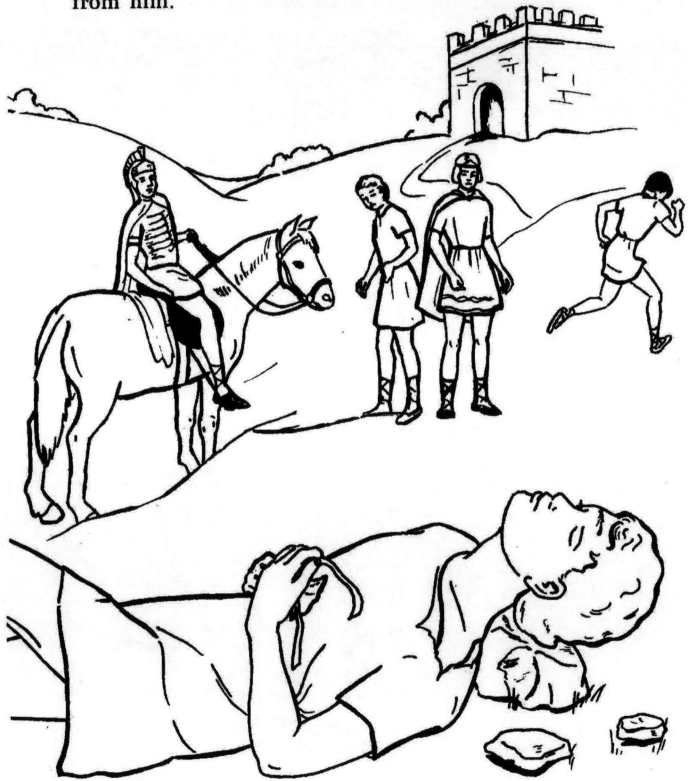

Tarcisius would not let them, so the boys killed him. Before he died he said, "I did not betray Jesus!"

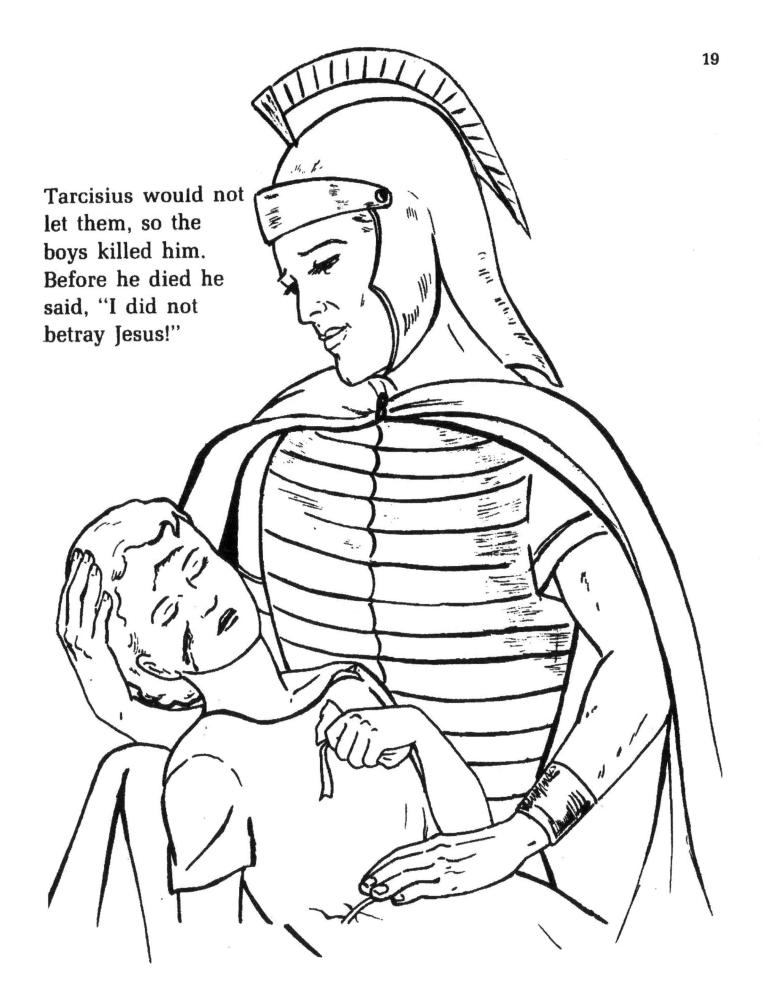

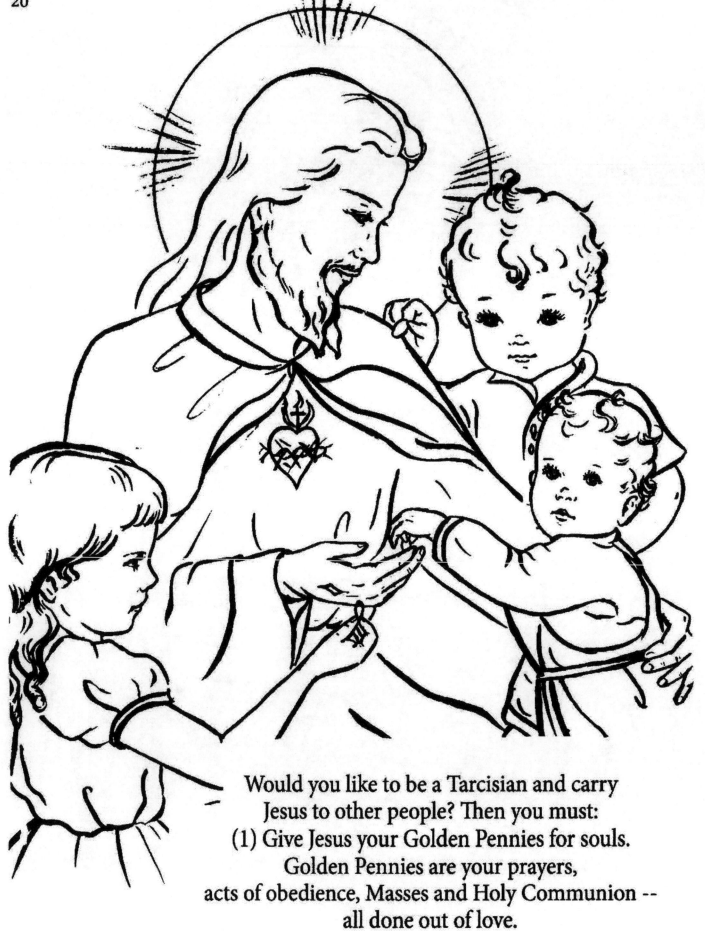

Would you like to be a Tarcisian and carry
Jesus to other people? Then you must:
(1) Give Jesus your Golden Pennies for souls.
Golden Pennies are your prayers,
acts of obedience, Masses and Holy Communion --
all done out of love.

(2) Tell others about the Golden Pennies.

22 Ask your parents to enthrone Jesus as King of your home. Jesus promised: "I will bless every home where My Heart is honored."

Jesus wants you to console
the Heart of His Mother by earning
Golden Pennies. Mary says:
"Say your Rosary to please Jesus."

MY FIRST FRIDAY RECORD

JAN.		APRIL		JULY		OCT.	
FEB.		MAY		AUG.		NOV.	
MARCH		JUNE		SEPT.		DEC.	

MY FIRST SATURDAY RECORD

JAN.		APRIL		JULY		OCT.	
FEB.		MAY		AUG.		NOV.	
MARCH		JUNE		SEPT.		DEC.	

MY NAME IS:

Made in the USA
Lexington, KY
21 June 2019